THE WISDOM OF
INDIA

Translated from the Tamil by
EMMONS E. WHITE

With Illustrations by
MAGGIE JARVIS

THE PETER PAUPER PRESS
Mount Vernon, New York

NOTE TO THE READER

Love and Religion are the two main subjects of India's ancient literature. These themes, especially religion, have powerfully affected her culture. What Western students have perhaps not always realized is that ancient Indian literature dealt not only with these two themes but also with *ethics*. In much of ancient Indian poetry counsel is given upon the subject of which moral qualities are essential and desirable, and which are undesirable or to be avoided. The wisdom of the Indian people, in this respect, is embodied in verses, each of which may vary from two to four or more lines, and also in the form of thousands of proverbs, or moral maxims.

Indian authors traditionally have chosen to deal in their works with the following four themes: Virtue, Wealth, Happiness (or Pleasure), and Salvation. The first three of these themes are essentially ethical, and the last only, religious in the usual meaning of that term.

Dr. G. U. Pope, a noted English scholar of the nineteenth century, has summarized these four themes in the following translation, adapted by the editor:

Virtue consists in Giving;
Wealth is that which is secured
Without wrong-doing;
Happiness results
When man and wife,
Sustained and sustaining,
Are one in love.
To renounce these three goods,
With heart fixed on God,
Is to experience
The bliss of *Heaven*.

E. E. W.

THE WISDOM OF INDIA

The Wisdom of India

One of the most noted of ancient classic poems dealing primarily with ethical subjects is the poem entitled "Tiru Kural" (The Sacred Couplets), composed about the beginning of the sixth century A.D. Many of the translations in this book are from that work. For centuries it has been reverenced by the Tamil people as one of their greatest classical works. Its opening chapter of ten couplets bears the title, "The Adoration of God." It seems appropriate, therefore, to begin our translations with a few selections from that chapter.

As in language "A" comes first,
So in the universe God is first.

They, who meditate unceasingly
Upon the majestic feet of Him

Who sits enthroned on the lotus flower
Which is the heart,
Will dwell forever
In highest heaven.

WHEN men attain the glorious feet
Of Him who is beyond desire,
Earthly trials will cease forever.

EXCEPT for those who grasp the feet
Of Him who is the Sea of virtue,
None can cross the sea
Of lust for pleasure and possessions.

THE head unbowed in worship
Before the God of perfect goodness
Is as useless a member
As a sense with no sensation.

THE TRANSITORY NATURE OF LIFE

THE wise realize that some day they will
have gray hair. Therefore, while young,
they refuse to be slaves to the world. But
those who try to remain young cannot

overcome their faults. They have no stability. At the end of their lives you will see them painfully trying with their canes to get upon their feet.

THE days fly past. Suddenly Death comes as though in anger. Therefore let man realize that wealth too will pass away, and let him begin now to lead a life of virtue.

WISE men know that the body is the seat of disease and sin. So let a man learn to live without enslavement to the body and in detachment from it, like drops of water on a lily leaf. Such men do not talk about this with others.

WHEN starvation comes, honor, high birth, learning, knowledge, almsgiving, the performance of austerities, high rank, industry, and the desire for women — all these will vanish.

SINCE life is but a bubble, wealth like wind-driven waves, and the body like letters written in water, why not turn to God?

FATALISM

In Indian philosophical thought the ideas of God, Fate and the Law of Karma seem to be inextricably interwoven.

Like the belief in God, the doctrine of fatalism means that man is not completely dependent on himself or that he is the captain of his soul. Fatalism implies that man feels that he is being acted upon by some power, not himself, which determines his destiny. The quotations which follow show how strongly Indian thought has been influenced by this basic idea.

If rainfall is scanty,
None can increase it.
If rain is abundant,
None can decrease it.
Likewise none can avert
The joys and the sorrows
He's destined to receive.

To those who meditate upon
Him of the Five Letters

Danger will never come.
This is also
The way of knowledge.
All other ways
Will lead to trouble.

If I think of some especial thing,
That or something else
Will come to pass;
Or, the thing I thought of
May or may not happen;
Or, a thing I never even thought of
May or may not come to pass.
All that happens to me
Is God's activity.

For those who overcome
The results of deeds
That are good or bad,
There is no need
For study of the Scriptures.
O my soul: be not troubled:
For those who have attained deliverance
There is no fate except
The imagination of the mind.

To distinguish not
Between good and evil,
And between the self and God,
Is man's ideal condition.
Searching for a God
Who differs from one's self
Is like cutting grass,
When offering sacrifice to God,
And looking for a cord
With which to bind it;
Not realizing
That same grass will serve.

THE LAW OF KARMA

No doctrine is more common in India's religious tradition, or has had a stronger hold upon the mind of the average Indian down through the centuries, than the Law of Karma.

Karma has been defined as "the effect of a person's acts upon his lot in a future existence." It is the law of moral retribution: namely, that all human actions, good and bad, have consequences which pursue

*the individual human being through a
series of rebirths upon earth. According to
this law, each individual must "eat the
fruit of all his actions." Such a dogma is a
rather clever rational attempt to account
for the apparently unfair distribution of
prosperity and disaster in human life. It
was an attempt to solve the perennial prob-
lem of evil.*

THEY who in love praise God unceasingly
will never encounter the consequences of
their good and bad deeds.

THEY that swerve not from the righteous
path of the God, who has subdued the five
senses, will not undergo rebirth but prosper long.

THOSE who attain a knowledge of the
Deity will successfully cross the ocean of
rebirth and reach the other shore. All
others will perish.

JUST as a calf will easily find its mother in
a herd of cows, so the deeds of one's life

will hunt him out in his next life. In other words, the deeds done by a man in this life will have an unfailing effect upon his next one.

YOUTH, beauty and wealth abide not. Even when one sees this, if he does no single virtuous act in this life, all other goods will perish with the body.

EVERYONE desires prosperity.
Who made the wood-apple round,
And colored dark the thorn-tree fruit?
All joys and sorrows result
From one's actions, good or bad.

WOMAN, even though you dip a two-quart pail into the ocean, it will not hold eight quarts! In the same way, the securing of a husband and much property depends on how you behaved in a previous life.

O YOU stupid man! Do you imagine that you, instead of God, control events? Those who look for fruit on the magnolia tree may find only poison. All events are the outcome of the deeds in a previous life.

In the quotations given in this book, the word virtue (or dharma, its Sanskrit equivalent) is frequently illustrated in detail. The late Mahatma Gandhi, India's greatest man of modern times, is reported to have said that dharma is a very difficult word to translate into English. The Indian lexicon gives the following meanings:

"Justice, virtue, conduct according to the Shastras, charity or almsgiving, the duty prescribed for one's personal rank, nature, the characteristics of animals, and the inherent qualities in plants."

In general dharma may be taken to mean the doing of one's duty according to one's station in life and, also, the giving of alms to the poor. Dr. G. U. Pope has stated that, in his opinion, the word essentially means Love.

BE aglow for virtue's sake:
Quench the flame of anger's fire.

SINCE goodness doth produce
Prosperity and joy of Heaven,
What greater wealth
Can any man desire?

'TIS true morality
To be blameless
In the heart.
All else
Is empty show.

SAY not,
"We'll learn from books
The fruit that virtue brings."
Behold the difference
Between a man who rides
In a palankeen,
And him who carries it.

IF, without neglecting
Opportunities for doing good,
One does good daily;
His virtuous acts,
Just like a stone,
Will block the stream
Of his rebirths.

TRUE pleasure comes
From moral living.
All other pleasures
Are linked with trouble
And win no praise.

HE who listens to good reading;
And virtuously shuns
The delights of the five senses;
Who's free from outward
And inward bonds;
And proclaims to all
Salvation's way —
'Tis he who merits the title
Of moral excellence.

HE who shuns discouragement,
Nor seeks the praise of others,
Who guards himself from evil
And gives aid to others,
Who hearkens to the wise —
'Tis he who's fit to listen
To the words of virtue.

TRUTHFULNESS, patience, magnanimity,
Self control and impartiality,

Renunciation of possessions,
Freedom from worldly ties,
Penance and the doing of good,
Faithful performance of one's vows —
These are the ten kinds of virtue.

KNOWLEDGE

To go deep into the heart
Of any subject whatsoever,
By whomsoever it is presented —
That is the way
True knowledge comes.

WHATEVER be the nature
Of objects that appear,
That alone is true knowledge
Which penetrates their heart.

THEY who in this life
Learn from a teacher true
That which is the truth
Will attain unto the path
Wherein is no rebirth.

TRUE wisdom comes
When man attains

Removal of his ignorance,
The cause of his rebirth.

IF one can know Reality,
Which all things underlies,
And has the strength to live
By that which doth unloose
All earthly bonds;
For him no worldly troubles
Will ever come to pass.

ONCE there was a Brahmin whose enemy
was a hunter. One day the hunter saved
the Brahmin's life. Likewise there was a
king who had a pet monkey. The monkey,
not knowing what it did, killed the king.
These incidents prove that a wise man,
though considered an enemy, may become
a true friend; while an ignoramus, considered a friend, is a potential enemy.

LEARNING

BE thorough in your scholarship,
And let the lessons learned
Govern all your life.

ONLY the wise have real eyes.
But the foolish man
Has two sores in the sockets
Where his eyes should be.

THE scholar is famous because all like to associate with him. They languish when they cannot see him.

AS the poor man stands humbly
In the presence of the wealthy,
So the noble will seek knowledge
From men of learning.
They who crave not knowledge
Will remain ignoble.

AS the water of a well increases in proportion to the amount drawn, so learning increases with the effort put forth.

HIGHEST of all riches
Is the wealth of learning;
All other wealth will perish.

GREATEST of all riches
Is that which comes from listening
To learned men.

SEEK no food for your stomach
While you have the opportunity
To learn by listening.

LET him who knows not books
Listen to those who do.
Such learning is a staff
On which to lean in trouble.

THERE are those people who prefer eating
to listening to the wise. What does it matter
if such ignorant beings should live or die?

OUTSIDE his realm a king
Has no reputation:
But the fame of the scholar
Goes with him everywhere.

As there are trees which bear fruit but do
not blossom, so there are men who will act
without having to be directed. Talking to
a fool is like sowing seed which does not
germinate. Even though you take great
pains to explain things to a fool, he will not
understand.

GREAT SOULS

THE great are they
Who attempt hard things,
Which lesser men avoid.

No matter who eats it,
Sugar is not bitter,
Nor is margosa sweet,
Though eaten by the gods.
So the worthy and unworthy
Do not change their natures.

THE help given to a good man
Is like letters engraved on rock;
But help to loveless men
Is like letters writ in water.

As a rock bends not, but splits
Beneath a heavy load,
So great souls
Bow not before adversity,
Though it may mean their death.

'TIS good to see good people;
To listen to their words,
And speak of their good qualities

Is also good.
Best of all it is
To live with them
In close association.

MEN unfit for friendship
Are like the water fowl,
Which abandons a pond
After the water is gone.
Real friends are like the water lily;
They remain to share
Both prosperity and adversity.

THOUGH a gold vessel break,
The gold will remain;
But a broken earthen pot
Is valueless.
So it is with folk
Of fine appearance and character:
The great,
Unlike ignoble men,
May lose their fine appearance
But will retain their character.

As the lovely swan
Seeks within a lake

The beautiful lotus,
So noble men
Will seek their own kind.
As the crow flies hungrily
To the corpse on the funeral pyre,
So ignoble men
Will seek their own level.

THE venomous cobra
Lives in hiding,
But the harmless watersnake
Wriggles about
Fearless in the open.
So the deceitful in mind
Will hide themselves;
While the guileless man
Will freely move about.

AS a tree until cut down
Will give its shade to all,
So it is with the wise:
Though others do them evil,
Until they die they'll try
Their utmost to aid others.

As the moon seeks not
To remove its dark spots,
But stands high in the sky,
Banishing darkness;
So the virtuous
Dwell not on their own defects
But, in compassion,
Will relieve the needs of others.

As the whirlwind catches the straw
But cannot shake stone pillars,
So, not the wise but fools
Will be overwhelmed by troubles.

O WOMAN with rounded breasts!
Just as the moon
Sends forth her rays,
Whether waxing or waning;
So men of noble nature
Will render help to others
According to their means.

O WOMAN with the golden bracelet!
A man will not say,
"My father became poor
Because he gave to beggars,

So I'll not give to them!"
He's like the sapling
Underneath the banana tree
Continuing to bear fruit
After its parent dies.

THE HOUSEHOLDER

Hindu tradition taught that there are four stages of life through which every man should pass. Woman was not included in all of these stages, although her condition in life was always an honorable one. These four stages are: (1) the bachelor who at puberty is invested with the privileges and duties of manhood, (2) the householder with a family, (3) the hermit who, after his children are grown up, retires with his wife to a forest for a life of pious meditation, and (4) the ascetic, who renounces all worldly ties and possessions, takes up staff and begging bowl and goes on pilgrimages from temple to temple, worshipping God and seeking release from the cycle of re-births. In spite of this emphasis upon as-

ceticism, *the author of the Kural and the poetess Auvaiyar have seemed to stress the domestic life as of equal importance to that of the ascetic.*

THE ideal householder is one who helps youthful students, the hermit, and the ascetic.

THE duty of the householder is unfailingly to serve God, ancestors, relatives, guests, and himself.

THE domestic life of him who has the love of wife and children, and does his duty to others, is one of distinction and high character.

THE life of one who is upright and helps others to attain the way of virtue is of a higher order than that of the ascetic.

VIRTUE is inherent in the married state.
The life of the ascetic
Is also praiseworthy,
If others speak no ill of it.

SWEET it is to enjoy one's food in the presence of God, one's ancestors, relatives and guests. They who know no such enjoyment are like the stork, which gobbles down in solitude the fish which it has caught.

THE RELATIONS BETWEEN THE SEXES

In India's ethical codes a high value has always been placed upon chastity, especially among women. In the last section of the Kural the poet deals with the topic of sexual relations which are within the law and those outside. Only one verse is quoted from the latter section.

IF the housewife
Be of good character,
What will the home lack?
If she be not such,
Of what use the home?

WHEN the housewife knows
No other god but her husband,

And if she rises
Early in the morning,
Then, if she says, "Rain",
Rain indeed it will!

ONLY she
Who guards her chastity,
Who assists her husband
And protects
The good name of the family,
Who's mindful of her duties
And faithful in performance,
Will receive a woman's praise.

OF what use are prison walls
To protect a woman's virtue?
The woman's possession
Of a firm mind
Is her best protection.

THE learned say
That the wife's chastity
Is the good fortune of the home,
And that good children
Are the home's decoration.

A WIFE's beauty lies in the fact
That she contradicts not her husband
Nor other dignitaries.

THERE is suffering for the fool
In the wisdom of the wise;
Suffering also comes
To those who love not virtue;
To the slender banana tree
The bearing of fruit means death;
And unseemly conduct in a wife
Means trouble for her husband.

THE folly of lusting
For the wife of another
Will not be found
Among those who know
The quality of virtue
And the nature of wealth.

AMONG all who walk
In a depraved way,
There is no greater fool
Than the man
Who stands in the doorway

34

Of the house of another,
Lusting for his wife.

THEY who commit sin
Against the wife of a friend,
Even though they appear to live,
They're really dead.

HATRED, sin, guilt and fear
Will never quit
The man who oversteps
The bounds of decency
In approaching another's wife.

IF you ask, Who are the men
Fit to receive rewards
In a world surrounded
By the terrifying ocean,
It is the men who touch not
The shoulders
Of the wives of others.

THE false embrace
Of money-loving courtesans
Is like to that of pallbearers,

Who for money embrace
A corpse in a dark room.

To use the prostitutes of the full breasts
for pleasure is like descending into a river,
floating upon a stone for grinding rice. It
will destroy wealth and end in poverty.
Therefore it is good neither for this life nor
for that which is to come.

O WOMAN of the dazzling bracelet: Just
as the crab, shellfish and banana tree produce offspring, pearls and fruit, and then
rot; so men, when wealth, wisdom and
learning decline in them, begin to lust after
other men's wives.

*The author of the Kural, Saint Valluvar,
evidently had a model wife; for, after her
death, he composed the following beautiful poetic tribute:*

Sweet as my daily food, O full of love,
O Wife!
Obedient ever to my word; chafing my
feet;

The last to sleep, the first to rise,
   O gentle one;
By night, henceforth, what slumber to
   mine eyes!

Tr. by G. U. Pope

THE GIFT OF CHILDREN

No finer gift could come to man,
Among all goods he might obtain,
Than to have children who are able
To learn the lessons that are needful.

IF one has children
Of blameless character,
He will not reap
The fruits of evil deeds
Even in seven rebirths.

SWEETER than ambrosia
Are the hands of little children
Held up for food.

SWEET is the music of flute and lute
To those who know not the melody
Of their little ones' prattle.

AMONG mankind in all the world
The thing which causes joy
Is, that one's own sons should be
More learned than one's self.

IF you ask,
What is a father's reward?
It is that they who note
The learning of the son
Will ask, "What deeds of merit
Has the father done,
To reap from Karma
So fine a fruit?"

THE mother and the father
Are the first gods
That children know.

CHILDREN, who anticipate
And obey their parents,
Are like the food
Of immortality.

THERE is no greater counsel
Than the words a father speaks.

LOVE AND FRIENDSHIP

*In the following verses love refers pri-
marily to relationships with one's own
family, kindred and social class.*

Is there any bar
To love's expression?
The tearful eyes of lovers,
Beholding a loved one's sufferings
Are love's true revelation.

To him who has no love
All things are for self;
To him with love for others
Even his very bones
Belong not to himself.

THEY say that the union
Of human life with body,
Whose bones are its foundation,
Is but the fruit of fusion
Of love with moral conduct.

LOVE for kin begets
The desire for others.

This in turn begets
The value called friendship.

THEY who incarnate
Love within the home
Will be rewarded
With bliss in heaven.

As the sun shrivels
The spineless worm,
So God will punish
The man who has no love.

WHEN there is no love
Deep within the heart,
What will be the use
Of the body's members?

A LOVING body
Is a living body:
A body without love
Is but skin and bones!

THERE is no greater gift
Than that of friendship.
There is no better guard
Against the acts of enemies.

FRIENDSHIP is not bounded
By country, race or long acquaintance.
To be one in understanding
Is quite enough for friendship.

TRUE friendship lives not
In outward smiles of greeting,
But in the smiles which well up
From a loving heart.

MAKE friends of those whose friendship is
like that of the dog, rather than that of the
elephant. Even though an elephant has
known its master for a long time, it may
one day kill him. But a dog, even when his
master has thrust a spear through its body,
will still affectionately wag its tail.

THOUGH one associates long with other
people, if they are uncongenial, there will
be no friendship. True friendship cannot
be annulled by separation.

SOME folk are like the Betel tree:
Their friendship must be cultivated
Daily or it will fail.

Others are the friends
Who resemble the Cocoanut tree,
Needing constant care
In the early stages only.
Best of all are the friends
Who, like the Palmyra tree
Planted on a sandy plain,
After the first day bears fruit,
And needs no further care.

No matter how friendly
You may act toward them,
Some people will never
Become your warm friends.
Although you heat milk,
Its flavor remains.
Though the sea-shell be burned,
'Twill still give forth whiteness.
So the noble in adversity
Will still remain noble.

IT'S the disease in the body
Which kills off a man;
It's the medicine which comes
From distant hills that cures.
So think not that your family

Will be the ones to help you;
It's the neighboring folk
Who may come to your aid.

O WOMAN of the flower-crowned hair! As the husk, separated from the paddy, loses some of its strength; so when two friends long separated become reunited, something of the firmness of their former relationship is lost.

HOSPITALITY

One of the chief requirements of the householder is that he be hospitable toward all who come to him. Even in the houses of the poor in many an Indian village it is an unwritten law that, whatever the condition of his house, the host will always hasten to provide for his guest the best of which he is capable. It should also be borne in mind that this hospitality consists, not in furnishing all sorts of amusements, but simply such bare necessities as food, shelter and clothing, and that these are extended to relatives, friends and strangers alike.

44

THE purpose of a home
With wife, children and possessions,
Is to provide the guests
With both aid and hospitality.

EVEN though what's eaten
Be the food of immortality,
It is unfitting to eat alone
While guests are waiting
Outside the home.

THE life of him,
Who daily entertains
The guests that come,
Will never meet with poverty.

IF one first feeds his guests,
Then eats what is left over,
For him will be no need
To plant the fields with seed.

HE who entertains
The guests who come to him,
And all who follow after,
Will be a welcome guest in heaven.

46

THE value of hospitality
Is measured by
The value of the guests.

THE distinction of being
A man of wealth
Is that he protects his relatives
When troubles come.

To have relatives at hand
To share one's joys and sorrows
Is the glory of life.

WORDS FITLY SPOKEN

LET what you speak
Behind another's back
Be the same
As what you say
In his presence.

LET your words to others
Be sweet to their ears.

NON-VIOLENCE

*Mahatma Gandhi made the doctrine of
non-violence famous in his day. The Kural*

has a chapter each, on the subject of killing and of doing harm to life. The existence of the doctrine of non-violence (Ahimsa) does not mean that there have never been any homicides in India. Homicides still take place there in spite of the prohibitions against murder.

The literal meaning of "Ahimsa" is to refrain from causing pain to anyone. Actually it includes the positive virtues of kindness and love toward all forms of animal life. The adherents of Jainism carry this doctrine to even greater extremes by interpreting it to mean doing no harm to very small forms of life such as insects! But they would not go so far as to include vegetable life, for that would make it impossible for man to live! It is quite essential for people of other cultures to realize that there is no understanding of India's religious traditions without an understanding of Ahimsa. It is probable that the veneration of the cow is partly due to this doctrine.

THE essence of virtue is
To refrain from taking life;
Murder is conducive
To all other sins.

SCHOLARS affirm
That if man shares his food
With hungry living creatures
And also protects them,
He performs the greatest
Of all acts of virtue.

To abstain from killing
Is the first of virtues.
Next comes truthfulness.

To refrain from killing and eating
The flesh of what is killed
Is the highest type
Of the ascetic life.

OF what value is knowledge
Of things as they are
To those who regard not
Others' troubles as their own?

49

WHY should he, who knows
The troubles that men make,
Himself be the cause
Of troubles to others?

THOUGH he should lose his life
By not slaying his enemy,
The ascetic will not kill.

How can he, who eats meat
To nourish his body,
Acquire the grace of love?

IT is impossible for one to keep material possessions if he is unable to protect them. In the same way, it is impossible for one to live in the way of love if he forsakes it by eating meat.

HE who carries a weapon has a mind only to kill. Likewise, he who has acquired the taste for the flesh of a living creature has a desire only for its flesh and not to protect its life.

WHAT is love but to refrain from taking life? The opposite of love is murder. Love

is not present when one eats the flesh of
that which has been killed.

LIVING creatures can be secure
Only if people do not eat them.
Hell swallows men
Who eat such flesh,
And never lets them go again.

To those who kill all kinds of good
Salvation's way is open still;
For him who murders gratitude
There is no saving way.

IMPARTIALITY

*Among the many virtues ascribed to the
householder none is more important than
that of impartiality. He is always just in
his dealings with others.*

To behave with impartiality,
Toward neighbor, friend and foe,
Is the height of virtue.

THE wealth of the impartial man
Will perish not but give
Strength to his posterity.

WEALTH and possessions accrue
From deeds of a previous birth.
To noble folk
Unswerving impartiality
Will be their chief adornment.

LET each one know within his heart
That if he should stray
From the path of justice,
Ruin will be his lot.

MEN of noble character
Will not regard as evil
The poverty that befalls
Him who stands firm
In the path of impartiality.

LIKE weighing scales
That balance evenly,
Impartiality,
Which leans not to one side,
Will be luster to the wise.

UNLESS justice
Be rooted in the mind,

It will not live
Within the spoken word.

WHEN inordinate desire
To steal another's goods
Is transformed into action,
The result is endless woe.

THEY who lust to steal
Cannot live nor prosper
Within the bounds of morality.

TRUTHFULNESS

WHAT is truthfulness?
It is the kind of speech
Which in no wise ways
Does harm to others.

IF man's speech agrees
With the truth within the heart,
He will surely live
In the hearts of all the world.

THE greatest human glory
Comes from truthfulness.
It causes no bodily suffering,
But will lead to every virtue.

OUTWARD cleanness
Comes from water;
But inward purity
Is known by truthful speech.

NOT all light
Illuminates well;
Light for the wise
Is truthfulness.

ANGER

THE control of anger
Is the beauty of austerity.

HE who prevents
Anger from mounting
Will succeed
In combatting it.
If anger does not arise,
What difference does it make
To control or not control it?

IF one becomes angry with another who is
stronger than he, he harms himself only.
And though his anger should temporarily

succeed, the result will be sin and evil.
There is nothing more harmful than anger.

SINCE anger is the cause
Of all evils befalling man,
One should forget
To be angry at anyone.

IS anything more cruel or hateful
Than the anger which destroys
The smile upon the face
And the love within the heart?

IF one would really guard himself,
Let him beware of anger,
Or it will destroy him.

THE fire of anger,
Which burns up
All that comes near,
Will also burn up
The pleasant raft of friendship.

EVEN though a wise man
Be harmed by an angry person,
He will not retaliate.

LET those who esteem us
And those who trample on us
Pass by! What though a fly
Crawl upon one's head?
'Tis well that the wise,
Who know its insignificance
Should not be angry.

BECAUSE the word of him
Who opens his mouth
And speaks unguardedly
Will burn him unceasingly:
The wise who continually listen
And ponder well
Will speak no heated words,
Even though they become
Dark with wrath.

WHEN confronted by the narrowminded
Who speak unseemly words,
Wise men will not flush with anger.
But small men will brood
Over such words:
Will rave about them
To the whole town,

And dash their heads
Against a post!

PATIENCE

THE earth calmly endures
Even those who defile it;
They wear virtue's crown
Who patiently endure
When others revile them.

BETTER to forget
The evil deeds of others
Than merely to endure them.

To be too poor to render hospitality
Is the poverty of poverties;
But the bearing of wrongs
Done in ignorance
Is the strength of strengths.

REVENGE upon a wrong-doer
Brings only one day's pleasure;
For him who bears with patience
Evil from another
There will be praise
Until the world shall end.

OVERCOME by patience
Those who act
From overweening pride:
Thus doing good for evil.

O LORD of the cool mountains clothed
with waterfalls! Argue not with a fool! If
you do talk with him, he will twist your
words in reply. 'Tis best if possible to slip
away from him.

THEY who guard themselves by knowledge, who fear what should be feared, and
use their abilities to bless the world; will
never suffer woes.

DESPISE not patient folk
Who may appear ignorant.
Note the patient, motionless stork
Which stands on the bank of a pond,
Waiting for its prey, the fish
To swim near.

IF you keep looking for faults,
At last even your relatives
Will leave you.

KINDNESS AND GENEROSITY

The ancient Indian poets stressed the virtues of kindness and generosity. Perhaps this was because of the great human need arising from the frequent failure of seasonal rains. The word in the Kural for "grace" can also be translated "kindness." It is frequently taught that kindness is to be shown to all living creatures. This is distinctly a Jain doctrine and is an evidence showing that the author was strongly influenced by that religion.

GREATEST of all forms of wealth
Is the wealth of kindness.
Material goods are riches
To fools only.

THEY who seek
The virtue of kindness
Must practise it.
It will be found
That kindness should be shown
To all life upon the earth.

THEY whose minds
Are filled with kindness
Will never enter
A world dark with woes.

No fearful evils
Will e'er overtake
Him who protects
All living beings
And is kind to them.

THE wise say that men
Who do cruel deeds
Are those who neglected virtue
And forgot the troubles
Which came to them in consequence.

THEY who became poor
Because of evil deeds
Can attain prosperity
After fulfilling their destiny.
But unkind folk will perish
And never become great.

EAT only after giving alms.